Shattered Trust to a Healed Heart

Earnestine Brown – Lewis

Dedication

I dedicate my book to my loving children, family members, and, most of all, to Jesus Christ, as well as to everyone who will find help through this book.

Acknowledgment

I am extremely grateful to God and my loving children for my success. The completion of my dissertation would not have been possible without their support and nurturing. I can't begin to express my thanks to my daughters, who are strong yet very appreciative. I would also like to extend my sincere thanks to my sisters, and I must thank my brothers as well.

About the Author

Earnestine Brown-Lewis is the CEO of Brown's Cleaning Services LLC, a notary in the state of Michigan, and an ordained minister.

Preface

This is a woman's journey who has witnessed many trials and tribulations. Life treats some people well, while others have to endure hardships to become strong.

For our narrator, the latter has been the case. Anxiety and past experiences gathered around her, trailing her like specters. Her past lovers, family, and friends have shaped her into who she is today and taught her valuable lessons. Her tragedy makes her the person she is today. Her attitude, prayers, and experiences shape her personality to be bold enough to face any obstacle.

Our past shapes us and prepares us for our future. This autobiographical recollection is a testament to this fact, as our narrator will see herself changing in the face of her childhood traumas and relationship issues.

Through the abyss of all the negativity in her life, the light of God and faith pulled her into redemption and safety. Faith reminded her how, amid hatred and breaching of trust, there is God on the other side, holding onto the string of hope wand anticipating His men to realize that all they have to do is pull it.

Contents

Chapter 1: Innocence Lost

Life is a collection of experiences that spread into our bodies and make us who we are today. As a forty-year-old woman, I watch my own life unfold like a haunting cinematic experience where a reflection of myself, much younger and vulnerable, is collecting one trauma after another: enduring pain, agony, and loneliness. The experience is quite solitary, with no one around to perhaps see the hurt in my eyes or the tears in the apparition of my younger self.

Broken, distorted, and frightened, I wonder how the consequences of traumatic events and nightmarish instances have altered my brain. So here, I fill the pages of this autobiography in the ink that has driven the power in me to reveal my story. A story of how I turned out to be the woman I am today. And then, perhaps, some reader might be able to witness the miserable circumstances unfold in front of a young and frightened girl whose childhood was stolen from her at a very tender age.

I was a typical, creative child, and I remember my early years as being joyful. With nine siblings to keep me from getting bored, I grew up in a relatively stable family from birth. Up until the night my childhood norm was taken away from me, I had a decent upbringing with a mother who was emotionally present.

The incident.

I can only describe this incident using the analogy of a broken mirror. Cracks surrounding the glass distort the reality depicted in the mirror. Each crack, edging in painful experiences, characteristically lies in the mirror and can never be eliminated from it.

The original state is lost.

One jolt and what once was a fully functioning mirror, unified in form, becomes a broken mess, never to retain its fine surface.

This broken mirror that sustains cracks of trauma is how I see that young girl after her innocence was lost entirely. It was flung into the shallow grounds of molestation while the world watched her in silence and did nothing about her state.

The joy that used to beam from my smiles disappeared. The reality of trauma and those who opted to silence my voice against it destroyed me.

I was three, and it was nighttime.

I was awakened by the terror of my older brother, who was trying to make me shower. As a young kid who only knew her safety net was maternal, I tried to wake my mother up, but she didn't budge. Her affection for her kids had noticeably decreased, so I couldn't rely on her to wake up anymore. Not from her sleep at that moment and not to face the reality of the pain her children were going to endure in their youthful years.

Frightened by the danger surrounding my brother's odd demand, I was forced to go through with it.

I was a three-year-old girl. A child who didn't even know the reality of molestation, let alone predatory behavior. And that moment, when my excuse of a brother stood by my door to witness his younger sister shower, the reality of molestation consumed me.

I didn't know what to say about this horrible experience. I was too young, naïve, and vulnerable to understand the enormity of the situation.

It was brutally and severely unfair.

Recalling this experience still feels like an endlessly occurring nightmare. It reopens the wound I've been struggling to close for years. I remember him standing by the bathroom door, creeping on me like a maniac. At that moment, being young and vulnerable, I was confused by his request. Before I could even comprehend the reason behind his horrifying presence, he asked me to wash my hair. Being younger than him, I gathered the courage to do as I was told.

Even at such an age, I knew what was happening to me was wrong. Something seemed very odd and wrong. What was frightening me at the moment while washing my hair was my mother's reaction. When I woke up the next day, unable to comprehend the reality of the previous night's incident, I got a beating from my mother. She noticed that my hair was ruined due to reckless washing, and fury overtook her. She ignored my attempts for an explanation and maybe even the nightmare I had experienced, choosing instead to hold onto circumstantial evidence.

"Your son touched me last night," I mustered up the courage to elaborate on it.

"What, son?" her ignorant response shattered my ability to speak up about the truth, leaving me in tears.

Even as a child, I knew that what had happened to me was severely wrong. I had been violated, yet my mother chose to laugh it off.

"My older brother, your son,"

"He would do nothing like that," Her confidence in the purity of her son was unmatched.

But so was the reality of what I had felt.

I felt disgusted and hurt at her unsympathetic attitude towards such a life-altering incident. A mother is supposed to protect her children and shelter them against predators. My mother, instead, sheltered the very predator who sucked the life's joy out of me. He consumed my purity, my childlike wonder, and the love I had for my mother.

After this incident, my mother and I became distant. She, to protect herself from the complications of child molestation, and I, for the sake of the little peace that was left within me. She had become reckless, avoiding the responsibility of her children.

This horrible incident left unfortunate marks on the fundamental grounds of my childhood. I couldn't even feel safe at my own house, and so my trust issues were enveloped by that night's incident. I couldn't trust anyone, my family, or others. These trust issues left me stranded in the solitary confinement of my own making. I had no one to ask for help. As a child, the protection I was assured of was never provided.

Loneliness and isolation were my only companions and my shadow, my only follower. I fell deeper and deeper into this pit hole of depression and the nightmarish reality that surrounded me every single day: a distant, careless mother, a sexual predator of a brother, and siblings who were too young and naïve to understand.

My defensive attitude toward danger triggered the isolation. I knew that I could never hurt myself; hence, loneliness treated me the way I once expected my family to treat me with respect and sympathy. I would never face my brother when he was at home. Being fond of loneliness and bearing the trauma of molestation, I used to lock myself in the room with my sister when he was around. My mother's negligence had given room for him to abuse us further.

Evil doesn't end after one act if it is present in someone. Having an evil heart, my brother mistreated his younger siblings. With no maternal shelter and paternal sympathy for us to seek help from, we became victims of his torments. It began with blowing weed smoke on our faces, leaving us a pit of cough. Gradually, it got worse. His evil slowly revealed itself through his acts. At the tender age of three, he forced alcohol down our throats and made us smoke weed.

My younger brother was just two while my sister was a year old when he blew weed smoke in their faces while forcing my brother to smoke a joint. Alcohol and drug abuse in children can have serious health and psychological impacts on them. Being a victim of drug and alcohol abuse, I can hold myself, along with my siblings, a testament to this statement.

We were helpless young children who were being tackled by an older man who knew no good.

His Old English 800 bottle never seemed to leave his lips. At home, he was usually drunk, swinging the bottle around and ready to pacify his vulnerable siblings with liquor. Pouring it up to the brink, he made us drink whole cups of beer and alcohol. At the time, he would tell us that it would help us sleep well. Noise irritated him, so he would make us gulp down these drinks.

He wasn't the only one who was drunk around the house. My mother, already absent, was a drug addict and an alcoholic. Bad habits were like a disease that consumed our house. As a child of an alcoholic, unpredictability and a lack of safety becomes a norm for you. I never felt sheltered. The place that I lived in couldn't be called a home; it was simply a house that gave room to neglected children and abusive adults.

A normal childhood includes exploration, good memories, and excitement. Mine had none of that. I mentally grew up, defended myself, and cooked for my siblings. My broken house didn't leave any space for childhood hobbies. With the presence of an absent mother and an abusive brother, I had no choice but to leave my happy days behind. So, when I was five, I knew how to cook, clean, and care for the family. I was never given the shelter of a home that prioritized the health and happiness of kids. Childhood was stolen from me at an age when I didn't even know that childhood was supposed to be the happiest time of one's life.

Children play games and display their creativity and childish wonder through those games. The only games we were accustomed to were created by a vicious, predatory adult in our lives, and that was my older brother. One game in particular was called Frog, in which he got to punch us and push us into a lake. This abuse went on as our parents, even when told, decided to brush it off.

We were alone. As young and vulnerable kids, we were the perfect targets of these monsters who pacified our voices and left out trauma for us to resolve for the rest of our lives. I did end up trauma bonding with a girl as I had no one around me to share my problems with. Being one of the very first friends that I had made, I trusted her with my soul. She heard me out and respected my story, so I gave her all my broken heart's love. Unfortunately, she further diminished my trust in people by turning her back on me and blackmailing me with the information she had regarding my life. I felt severely betrayed. The only person I found friendship and loyalty in broke my last trust in the world. It was awful. But fate somehow opened a gate for me, and we moved away from her, hiding away her secrets in my heart and mine in hers.

Trust and friendship never occurred to me; I was a broken and abused child who was only used to nightmares. Even sleep had stopped providing me the peace I yearned for. The kind of calm I didn't know was normal in other people's lives. Only night terrors and tears met me in my sleep. With all that I had to endure, nightmares and insomnia were another struggle. Pained by my family, I was always on defense, which inadvertently affected my sleep. I no longer witnessed the glimmering happy dreams of a child. They were all nightmares, reminiscent of the abuse that I had to tolerate. My soul resided in a body that endured pain, patience, and depression.

Chapter 2: The Teenage Years

A life in which a child held the world's responsibility on her shoulders was none to admire. While I cared for everyone around the house and tried to keep things together, my young mind was never made for such burdens.

The glimmer of childhood I found lingered in the household of my female friend, whose mother treated me like her own daughter. Coming from a chaotic household with an ignorant and unavailable mother, I found her attitude to be very comfortably foreign. The years of spending time without maternal affection were finally found contained in the lap of my friend's mother.

I greatly admired her and finally learned what motherhood felt like to a child. Yet even before I could thoroughly enjoy it, this shelter was taken away from me. Her influence didn't wither away but was brutally snatched from not just me but my friend as well. I was horrified to learn at the age of twelve that her child's father killed her. He had slashed her throat repeatedly, causing her to quake in her final gasps of breath. The monster of a man only committed this horrific act because she did not return to him or reciprocate his advances.

This case wasn't just a wound that needed years of healing time but left my heart unguarded in a world of untrusted people. I had finally begun to let my guard down, and that's when unfortunate circumstances deemed my decision to be foolish.

So, still vulnerable and fragile from the experience, I had announced my lack of trust in people.

Even myself.

This mindset carried me into my teenage life. It was a phase of exploration, new love, and happiness for some children, but for me, it was as uncertain and unpredictable as the situation at my house. But carrying the soul of a broken 13-year-old, I lived my life one day at a time.

On May 29, 1993, I met my first husband. I, a teenager, and he, a 19-year-old, crossed paths on a fine day. I was walking my best friend to her house when I saw him. Infatuated by him at first glance, I fell for him at the tender age of thirteen.

Our love story soon blossomed into a date when we went out to eat at various restaurants. Young and vulnerable, I was impressed by his gift-giving and attention abilities. He provided me with the comfort I had once lost, making me believe he was the right match for me. He landed a firm place in my heart by giving me attention and lending an ear of sympathy. Something that I never found at my house.

What I had wanted the most at the time was to be noticed—the feeling of being alive while an audience acknowledges and appreciates your presence. My family had never given me that kind of love or attention that breathes life into people and gives them a reason to live. My husband, my boyfriend then, gave me reasons to exist and smile every day.

Hearing my problems out, he made me feel like I was visible, like a diamond lying behind the depths of rocks, patiently waiting to shine. At that age, it felt like it was my time to sparkle and be appreciated. Knowing my abusive family history, he was always ready to listen to me and protect me.

The trust that I had lost after my friend's passing slowly started to build up again. It was coming back around, and I was ready to accept peace and love with open arms.

So, our relationship was established with me spilling my heart out and him quietly listening and nurturing my broken heart. His caring attitude wasn't simply limited to emotional needs but academic ones as well. He helped me with my schoolwork and gave me the respect no one had ever offered to me. Respect was never a part of my life, so the feelings that erupted inside me were quite new and exciting. I was being heard, and I was turning into me again. A me that I had lost years ago, the first time my brother had abused me.

He introduced me to a lot of things and provided me with new thinking horizons and perspectives I never knew existed. Everything felt so new and different with him that I soon fell for him.

Our connection became stronger, and we slept together regardless of age. In June, the harrowing news of my pregnancy shattered my teenage years. I feel like fate opened this to me because God knew I had grown up quicker than normal kids. My younger days were spent catering to my siblings' needs and cooking them food, and now, at the tender age of thirteen, I was gifted with life. Knowing how mentally mature I was for my age, he treated me like an adult. And this news only brought further support my way. He cared for me and surrounded me with everything he thought I needed. The excitement of having a child consumed his demeanor, and happiness was quite evident on his face. His joy was contagious; he was overwhelmingly excited to tell everyone about my pregnancy.

Aligned with his celebrations was my enjoyment of my motherhood. Though I found it at an early age, I was always used to providing maternal affection, and motherhood came to me naturally. Now, surrounded by my children, I know I couldn't have asked for anything better. I have always protected them from predators and people I knew wouldn't treat them well. As for my initial stages of motherhood, people around me were quite unsupportive.

My own mother decided to kick me out, and I was left to stay with my mother-in-law. Our differences made it harder for me to adjust to her house, as we spent most of our time arguing. Sustaining my peace became harder each day with her presence.

The date is still etched in my mind: June 1, 1994.

I had moved in with him and his mother, and that's when all the abuse began. It started with him getting home after a bad day and pouring all his anger on me. The stress of being the family's sole provider ended up consuming him. I, being so used to abuse, just endured all the pain. As the woman of the house, I believed that I persevered for my children.

All the pain I had to deal with was only tolerable because of my children. They brought me joy, peace, and happiness. My wounds were healed through their enlightened presence. Being the best part of my life, they provided me with space to breathe and be happy. If it wasn't for them, I would have been dead.

For years, I had to tolerate the brutality of my husband and his mother, and yet my shell didn't break. I didn't have any job at the time or the financial means to shelter my children and myself. My plans to escape soon started to occur to me, and I devised a way out of this spider web.

It wasn't easy, though; I had known this man for years, and all the giddy feelings attached to him consumed my mind. The physical and mental abuse that I had to go through was too substantial for me to pay any more heed to the love I had left for him.

My feelings were brought to finality when fear replaced them. In 1997, he shot my brother in the stomach with a 12-gauge shotgun. It so happened that my brother's girlfriend and my boyfriend got into an argument, and she pulled out her gun. To reciprocate with violence, my boyfriend did the same. My boyfriend ended up shooting my brother because he was defending his girlfriend. This incident consumed my love for him, and maternal instincts overpowered my mind. I could only see the safety of my children, and so, at the age of 18, we broke up. I was no longer going to be with a man who could shoot someone.

Geographical distance also eased my fears, and he moved up to Alabama, leaving me as a single parent of four kids. Financial unpredictability plagued my mind then, so, with a broken heart, I searched for a house and a job.

Since our divorce settlements weren't based on any financial security, I knew I had all the responsibility for my children and myself to carry.

History felt to be repeating itself as I once again found myself alone, in a maternal position (though this time literal), looking for a shelter. Stress was a hauntingly real feeling that had diseased my mind then. In normal circumstances, divorces and breakups have to be emotionally dealt with. My case, being unfortunately different, brought loneliness my way.

After some time of navigating my way through corporate struggles, I found a house and a job. Happiness was slowly becoming a possibility for me. Picking up the pieces of myself that he shattered, I was working on myself and sustaining the livelihood of my kids.

That was until a horrible incident descended upon me.

I was dealing with a man who used to stalk me every day. Not paying attention to his alarming moves, I chose to ignore him. As a 19-year-old, I was quite naïve and chose to ignore his obsession with me. He had been watching me for over a month, navigating my every move. He knew when I got in and out of work yet chose to stalk me in silence. It felt a little creepy, but I let it slide since I was too consumed with my work and motherly responsibilities. Looking back, I realized this was the biggest I could ever make.

One tiring day in October, a week before my birthday, I came home to experience something very traumatizing. I was already quite exhausted from work and quite unaware of what would happen to me. I had no idea he was watching me from my yard, hiding behind the bushes. He was waiting for the right moment.

And when it came, I felt a gun against my temple. He threatened me not to make a sound and pushed me inside the house. I was in utter shock and horror as he walked me into the house and duct-taped my hands. Struggling to move, I watched this evil man reveal his true motifs.

He mentioned how he had been watching me from the very first day since our move and was waiting for the perfect moment to rape me.

Frightened, I tried my best to reason with a man who was speaking beyond human rationale. That's when he uttered that he was in love with me and, to my horror, knew all my children's names. This threat was enough for me to give in to his commands. For the sake of my children's safety, I let the trauma of being sexually abused haunt me once again.

Throughout the painful process, he kept the gun in his hand. And finally, when the torment was over, he said that he would kill me and my children if I called the police.

Being a single mother in a town full of strangers, I felt quite helpless at the hands of his threats. I was already a broken woman, and this incident flung my spirit into an abyss of darkness. The world came caving down upon me, but I still managed to report him. With the little courage that was left in me because of my children, I went up to the police for an investigation. They got me a rape kit and advised me not to work late. I was also told to be hyper-aware of my surroundings, which I stood by.

He committed this heinous crime in the same house that I had found in hopes of finding a spec of happiness in the pool of torment. In return, we only found more torment. Feeling lost in this world of strangers, I clung to my children for familiarity and decided to look forward to another chapter in life.

I was three months pregnant when they found him. That was when he received ten years in prison. Justice was brought to my purity, but this could never take me back to the state I was in before the trauma. The damage was done, and I had to learn from it for the rest of my life.

The next phase of my life spanned over a move. I, leaving the broken and traumatic shambles of my past, moved to Alabama. The cost of living was much cheaper as compared to Michigan. And so, hoping to forget every painful memory, I looked up to get my GED with four children by my side. I was pregnant with my fifth child at the time of the shift.

The incident of the rape had made me more vulnerable than ever. I was tired of carrying the burden of my broken existence alone. And loneliness seemed to be my worst enemy at the time. I never had a family I could embrace for comfort, so I peeped into the life of my ex, the closest person I could call family. We had been conversing for quite some time, and he wrapped his apologies in the comfort of promises. He told me that he would never hit me and that he would provide for my children and shelter and heal my wounds.

The tragedy of loneliness is that it leaves you no choice but to trust those who surround you.

I was exhausted and, on top of that, pregnant. So, a little skeptical, I decided to tie the knot with him on March 12, 1999. Throughout the wedding process, he sustained his promises, which provided me with a little comfort.

And so, with five children and a man I had no choice but to trust, encircling me with a ring of safety and promises, my teenage years ended.

Chapter 3: Marriage to Monster

After the honeymoon phase, I was afraid that my husband would immediately change. But, to my pleasant surprise, he remained the same. Sticking to his promises, he treated me and the kids right. He committed to his fatherly duties and tried his best to create new and healthy memories with his children. After years of being surrounded by an unpredictable environment, I finally settled in peace. I had a loving husband, a safe house, and children whose livelihood was connected to my breaths.

Life went by smoothly. Or at least it seemed to be that way for a while.

Eight months into our marriage, I stumbled upon a voodoo book that was hidden on the shelf of my son's room. Not paying much attention to it, I decided not to bring it up.

Looking back, I regret doing so because the mystery around this book still remains. After discovering that book, I noticed a change in my children. An uncertain eeriness to the environment that seemed so normal a little while back. I still believe that this man was practicing voodoo on us because our house had progressively become more rigid. He ran the house as a military base, being very firm and strict about the house and making us uneasy exercises.

Whenever he liked, he would call a meeting and ask us to do jumping jacks, push-ups, and other exercises that required a lot of strength. It almost felt as if he thrived off our struggles.

While he treated the kids well, his rigidity sometimes felt a little suffocating. I remember him spending time with the boys playing ball while he taught his daughter how to ride a bike. His rules and his quality time had to include physical activities that sometimes weighed down my children's spirits. Nevertheless, we persevered.

His attitude was quite bearable to us until his criminal history and abilities started to unfold before him. It all began with his mysterious behavior, which progressively got worse.

I first learned about his criminal abilities when he got pulled over. He was in a truck with his brother, and he was arrested for soliciting a prostitute. This event caused him to be sent to jail along with his brother.

At first, I dealt with a lot of disbelief regarding this incident, but soon, anger towards myself for trusting him took over. While being true to his word, he still ended up ruining a perfectly good marriage.

After this arrest, his arrival back home was nothing but suspicious to me. He had become closed off and had started spending nights outside. We never got the chance to get intimate as he seemed to never be in the mood, and my worries increased.

It seemed as if he had stopped loving me. He never met my eyes when we talked, stopped kissing and showing affection, and limited his conversations with me. With such a dreadful change in his attitude, I feared his heart was elsewhere. And truth be told, reality did seem to be the case.

The only area where I found comfort was his financial aid. He responsibly gave me money and sustained our lifestyle by paying bills and providing the children with allowance. Unlike last time, when he did not take responsibility for the house, his attitude was more refreshing this time. Externally, everything seemed to be alright. He was paying the bills, caring for our needs, and spending time with the kids. But deep down, I knew that the person I was sharing my house with wasn't the same one whom I married. Something had changed between us, and I was fearful of discovering the reality.

That was when the reality came down upon me. It was a haunting day in the year 2012 when I first found out that my husband was a rapist. This news was unfathomably traumatizing. The incident happened on December 7, 2007, and I found this out years later. All my doubts and all the suspicion I had toward him had taken a horrifying manifestation. It was in the same year that he was arrested for rape charges.

Not thinking of any other option, I decided to go to his trial to see for myself who he had become. And the image was not a pretty one. A man with whom I had spent most of my life was sitting in his seat, yet I failed to find any familiarity. He was a monster, and I was tied to him with a ring that held the promises he had never kept up.

Looking at the victim, I couldn't help but relate to her miseries. It reminded me of my troubles in the past and made me empathetic. She was a woman, like any other, who was brutally raped by a senseless and animalistic man. Hearing her story made me believe every word that she uttered. I felt unfortunate for her and myself, who had kept my trust in such a man. It was, once again, shattered and spread in a million pieces. I was very triggered, and my trust in men had left me broken. It completely vanished, and I felt like my life was a waste. My teenage years were wasted struggling to find a safe place for my kids and me. My twenties also went down the drain, as I had never felt so down in my life. I had spent 18 years with this man and couldn't find a reason to sustain it any longer.

His prison life was a blessing in disguise for me because it gave me space to rebuild my life again. Once again, I found myself in the shambles of misery, but instead of giving up, I decided to pull myself out of those thorns. I needed to gather myself back again and rediscover myself. So, in every way possible, I attempted to do it. The one thing I have taken from the internal bruises I've received is that to heal, you need to look forward. So, instead of looking up at the clouds of misery that surrounded me, I looked forward at the grassy lands of freedom.

Rebuilding myself, I knew that I would have to do it alone. Since marrying my husband, I haven't talked to my family. So, the only sense of home I found in this world of strangers was church. I started going there after my children went to school. My children took the prison incident to heart. As my oldest son was living with me, he understood everything that had happened. And he was deeply disturbed by it. The kids at school had started picking on them. They openly called their father a rapist and shamed them for it. I was quite ashamed and prayed that the bullying would stop because they should never be the ones to suffer.

This very reason became another reason for me to hate their father. I started to despise him for whatever he had done. Children are innocent creatures, and they don't deserve this treatment. And I felt quite overprotective of my children, who had already been through a lot.

This phase of my life didn't simply weigh me down but my kids as well. And for this very reason, I turned to prayer. I would plead to God for hours to make me the perfect mother and father my kids wanted. They needed to feel safe, so I tried my best to provide them with a healthy environment. I prayed away, begging God not to let my emotions consume me.

Even with the positive mindset I had, I was not able to get rid of the unbearable nightmares that haunted me in my sleep. I was enveloped in anxiety and depression but never stopped looking at the sun and the brighter side of things.

I am a weak soul, so give me the capability to be strong for my children.

This prayer never left my lips. I needed the guidance of God more than ever in my life. I was a broken soul and tired of being betrayed by mankind; I needed a higher authority to shelter me in His love and influence.

The phase of a marriage with a monster ended with me close to God and stronger in my belief.

Chapter 4: The Road To Rebuilding

The first sign of progression is acknowledgment. Realizing the error of your ways leads you to broaden your horizons, seek help, and pray. That's what I did as well; after my messy divorce, I recognized my problems and started to find ways to fix them. Prayer and tears initiated the progress.

I craved connection with the Lord and attempted to rediscover the purpose in life that He had created for me. I recall praying, talking to God, and going to church regularly in hopes of getting a sign. A little glimmer of hope that would pull me out of distress. I had dedicated myself to my husband, but trust issues plagued my mind now that he wasn't in my life anymore. Phases of depression led me to question my new reality.

The reality without a husband.

I was left shattered with a lack of faith and trust in people. I had spent so much time with him, and for such horrific circumstances to occur scared me for my future. Alone in this world of liars and betrayers, I needed comfort for myself and my children. I also needed presence in my life, a light that couldn't be ignited by any random candle but the candle of faith. I needed the Lord. I pleaded to Him for answers. For Him to show me the way to my rightful destiny. A place where I would be able to find peace and happiness. I was stuck in questions and problems that I desperately needed to get out of. Memories of him and how he lied to me all these years were a painful reminder of the dreadfully evil side of human beings. And so, I pushed myself closer to God, knowing that He would provide me with answers.

And He did.

I knew what I had to do. Get me out of destructive cycles and navigate to a place where I could find peace. The only place that came to mind was my family.

No matter how enormous the differences are, the family is bound by blood.

It was through the Bible that I was able to find the truth. God has created purposes for every soul sent to Earth, and I discovered mine there. Phases of depression spiraled me into alcohol abuse and smoking. It was like I had nowhere to go, and loneliness was being sent to me as a curse. And within this wide abyss of depression, the light of God still managed to touch me. I decided to avert my gaze from mankind and give all my attention to God.

God permits alcohol, but excessive drinking is a sin. And rightly so, for there is no better fixture to problems than God's light.

"And do not get drunk with wine, for that is debauchery, but be filled with the spirit." (Ephesians 5:18)

This highlights the force of the light and the significance of God's influence. No destructive temporary escape can compete with faith and hope. It also reveals that moderation is favored in the Bible. Drinking with caution is not only biologically important but mentally and spiritually important. For reinforcement, it has been mentioned in Proverbs 20:1, 23:20, and Isaiah 5:22 to highlight the much-needed avoidance of alcohol.

The Apostle Paul, inspired by the Holy Spirit, instructs mankind not to get lost in the world of intoxication. There are instances where the Bible forbids alcohol, but there are situations when alcohol in moderation is acceptable.

Teenage drinking is not as grey as adult drinking. It is not only against the law but spiritually rejected as well. God commands us to obey laws like these for our own good.

"Everyone must submit himself to the governing authorities, for there is no authority except that which God has established." (Romans 13:1)

Laws are made to be obeyed, for they hide our benefits. Disobedience is discouraged not only for finding heaven but for the peace of our minds. In order to ensure peace in my life, I changed my ways. Instead of finding closure in alcohol and smoking, I flipped my life around and looked for the light of God. I made a list of things I wanted to cut out of my life, and on top of the list was alcohol. I created discipline in my life and slowly pushed cigarettes out, followed by avoiding drinking gatherings, and lastly, removed coffee from my life. This helped me get over my addictions and discover the person hidden behind all issues.

I walk by faith and not by sight.

This service to God did wonders to reignite the purpose of my life. And it was to take care of my children and live for my family. For anyone else who came into my life, I prayed for their intentions to be revealed to be revealed to me. I trusted God's judgment, and that pushed me away from a lot of ill-intentioned people.

Everything was watered down to a few people in my life. My children and my family, whom I had abandoned. I had left them to move on with my life but realized that I now needed them more than ever. Rebuilding the road of life led me back to my family. I reconnected with them, and we were quite happy. I was now grown enough to look past our differences and become one once again.

I reconnected with my siblings as I was able to put the past aside and appreciate the love we had for one another moving forward. I was able to forgive and forget because I was inspired by what the Bible tells us. It provides us with guidance to amending relationships. In *Matthew 18:15-17,*

"If your brother or sister sins, go and point out their fault, just between the two of you. If they listen to you, you have won them over. But if they will not listen, take one or two others along so that 'every matter may be established by the testimony of two or three witnesses.' If they still refuse to listen, tell it to the church, and if they refuse to listen even to the church, treat them as you would a pagan or a tax collector."

This highlights the importance of communication, forgiveness, and sympathy in relationships. If you do well with people, God will repay you with blessings.

With this sentiment, I knew what the right thing to do was.

The reconnection led us to make new and pleasant memories together. We went out and took various trips together, communicating more openly. Empathy strengthened our bond. I was no longer a woman scared of the outside world. I was free, functioning under the will of God, which helped me blossom in my relationship with them. They accepted my children with open arms. My family extended, and love multiplied, making me forget about my hardships and all the suffering. I was rebuilding my life with all the right tools.

They welcomed my children with open arms. The past has bruised me internally, but I no longer cared for how people had treated me. I was on the right path with the Lord's light shining upon me; therefore, I didn't need to hold grudges. When I saw the smiles on their faces and the genuine attitude beheld for me, I knew that I had made the right decision. I had prayed on it, and God had provided me with a way out of the mess my ex-husband had made.

I had a lot of things to learn again. How can I embrace happiness, trust other people and my intuition, and avoid harmful escape routes? My children and God were the only reasons I was alive at that time. I knew that the Lord had not made the human body to be put an end to. Life, though hard, can be beautiful as well. It can contain tiny illuminating moments of happiness that carry our reasons to survive. To wake up every morning, thank God for all His blessings, and work for Him. Each breath depends on His will, so we need to obey Him. And that I did. I went to church and prayed away, letting the feelings of discomfort wash away as I uttered the Lord's word. No longer was smoking or alcoholism filthy escapes for me; I had faith. I had transformed into a more stable and confident individual. I never let my issues come in the way of being the best version of myself.

My divorce had been finalized, and this new chapter in life was hopeful. I had moved back with my family in Detroit and was looking forward to working on myself and my children. I decided to explore different lines of work; the first thing that struck me was truck driving. I went to truck driving school for this passion and started a job as a truck driver to sustain a stable income for the household. I created a work-life balance to ensure that I spent time with my kids, being a soccer mom, and working as an efficient employee to be given promotions.

I had stopped living in the past and decided to flourish in the present and look forward to the future; it was the only way God had intended life to be. The pain of the past might be unbearable, but you have to learn how to live with it.

"No, dear brothers and sisters, I have not achieved it, but I focus on this one thing: Forgetting the past and looking forward to what lies ahead, I press on to reach the end of the race and receive the heavenly prize for which God, through Christ Jesus, is calling us." (Philippians 3:13-14)

New memories started unfolding as I settled into my new life with my children and family. My kids started their new venture, which included soccer. And I, being as interested in their athletic endeavors as them, supported them. My youngest two played it for five years, during which they received medals. I recall staying back for hours, watching those two have the time of their lives.

Whenever I missed one of their games, I would make up for it, for I knew that I was their mother and father for them. Therefore, I was their whole world and needed to be present in every little memory they created for them to look back. Once they become nostalgic for their childhood, they recall the support of their mom instead of someone who wasn't there for them.

We also started movie nights when we would gather pizza, popcorn, and candy and dine over a good movie. These little moments provided me with the kind of peace I never thought I would be able to gather. All I had to do was focus on the signs of God, accept the plan He had for me, and hope for the best. Being a single parent may scare many, but I knew I had the light of faith in my life.

As a single parent, I didn't let the anxiety of caring for my kids take over. Having them in my life was a blessing, and I made sure to express my love and appreciation to them. I didn't want what happened to me to affect my children's lives. They deserved better than that. My past no longer defined me, and I ensured it didn't remotely define my children. I wanted to be a role model, a strong and resilient woman to them. I bravely dealt with my traumas from the past so that I could provide my children with a life that I couldn't get.

"So do not fear, for I am with you; do not be dismayed, for I am your God. I will strengthen you and help you; I will uphold you with my righteous right hand." (Isaiah 41:10)

This verse throws light on how fear can always be eliminated by deep-rooted faith. If one believes in the light of God, one can overcome any fear and fight their demons with courage. God has given us the ability to overcome obstacles, and He wants trust and hope from us. These two are like puzzle pieces that fit perfectly into the frame of faith. It is through love that you can overcome fears. Through The Word of God, we can also capture inspiring stories of people losing hope but finding God's light to become the best versions of themselves and serve God's Kingdom. That is what I am here to do as well, serve.

We started going out more often as well. Family gatherings and other occasions brought a refreshing change in my life. I realized how much I had craved this support and love over the years. If you surround yourself with positivity, so much changes. Everything turns for the better if you surround yourself with positivity. It impacts your mental health. Support from family is important for self-improvement because you are reminded why you become a better person every day. Seeing my children smiling sent comfort through my body. It was a reminder of how I was winning at life. I had the Lord to thank for that. He pushed me out of the path of darkness and ignited faith in me. He also revealed new perspectives that made me a more sympathetic person. It made me more tolerant and forgiving.

Their hobbies and their academic achievements made me a proud mother. And in those moments, when I saw them running in the field and squealing in joy with their friends, I knew that I was made to be a mother. A mother who needed no shelter or sympathies of a man to care for her children. I was a strong woman with firm values who passed them on to her children. God gave me the strength to deal with everything that I did. Alongside being a soccer mom, I also worked for my family. We didn't need anybody to complete us. We were enough.

God had given me a chance at life, repentance, and creating happiness for myself. And so, at this phase of my life, I focused solely on rejuvenating my relationship with God and finding ways to pray more often. Religion created a path of a second life for me, a way to fix my issues and move along.

My trauma had turned me into a firm protector of my children. I knew there was always a possibility of people having ill intentions, so I cared for them and brought them up without anybody's help.

Chapter 5: Love, Betrayal and Loss

After slowly picking up the pieces of my broken life, I adjusted to being single and what that entailed. With God and family by my side, my life seemed complete. The path that I had chosen for myself brought me peace and comfort. The only thing that was missing from my life was the love of a partner. With the experiences from my past, I knew that I had to be more careful around love. It had let me down in the past, and I didn't want it to happen again.

Unfortunately, life had other plans for me.

I met my second husband years ago when I was still married. The attraction was there from the very first encounter, but I didn't pay much attention to it. Years later, when I was single once again, we hit each other on Facebook. It was ironic that my first husband had introduced me to him. Life can be quite coincidental in that respect. You never know how you get tied to people and situations. Circumstances that don't even occur to us happen and leave us processing reality.

From stumbling upon him at a family get-together to dating me, how quickly we bonded seemed surreal. Our story began in 2021 when he asked me to meet him. He told me that he was a driver, and we chatted about our careers and aspirations.

My defensive walls were mounted high enough to avoid heartbreak when I met him. I was on my guard the whole time when we first met. I was not ready to trust another man again and let him ruin my life.

Despite all of this, his words started to make my heart melt. The way he spoke was quite impressive. He somehow always knew what I needed to hear. I felt heard and understood. So, our conversations were never boring. Due to his ability to charm, I slowly started to let my guard. I felt comfortable and safe with him, so I followed my instincts and started to fall for him.

I was overjoyed by the idea of working on everything with him because he was someone who understood me. After some time of talking, he asked me to meet him in Alabama on July 3, 2022. He mentioned how he had liked me for a long time and loved talking to me. This brought warmth to my heart. Someone was finally seeing the real me and was accepting it with open arms.

We met on the amazing evening of July 6 in Alabama, and the night ended with our endless conversations. It was beautiful, and my heart felt full of love. He was very good at flattery, and he used that ability on me to impress me further.

He took me around for dates and treated me chivalrously. On our ride back to his house, we talked about our aspirations and how we wanted to spend our lives together. It was very peaceful to have that conversation because it indicated that he was a dedicated man.

Spending time with him alone was fine. When his cousins came over to his house, I started to feel uncomfortable. It was a party of thirty people, and they had brought alcohol and weed with them. The loud party and the crowd started to tire me out. I tried my best to compose myself, but partying wasn't really on my mind as a mature woman. I just wanted to relax and have a good time with him.

The party went on all night, and at 6 AM, I was exhausted. I wanted to sleep, but he insisted on being intimate. And considering how well he was doing regarding affection and showering compliments, I gave in, and we shared the bed for the night. We were so exhausted that we only managed to wake up at 4 PM when there was a knocking on the door. Quickly dressing up, we joined his family once again.

His cousins were party people, and the next day, after spending time on a date, we had to go back to their drinking parties again. I was again put in an uncomfortable position but had to tolerate it because of him. He treated me so well that dealing with these overbearing parties didn't seem much to me. That aside, I had started to ask him to avoid excessive drinking. My past with drinking and drunkards abusing me still haunted me, so I didn't want that to be repeated. Hence, I kept advising him against it. He, thankfully, listened and only drank beer, getting to bed at 2 AM. He told everyone that he had something important to do in the morning and that he went to bed with that. We showered together, and our night came to an end.

We woke up to an adventurous day. He first took me out for breakfast, then went to the salon to get my nails done. We then went to the barber's, where he got a haircut.

Everything was at his expense, which made me feel very important.

On our way back, he asked me if I was uncomfortable with his behavior the previous night. Being good at communication, he already knew that I was. So, he assured me of never drinking again. The idea of him changing for the better just to make me happy flattered me a lot.

Following this conversation, he told me he had a surprise for me on Monday. It was a beautiful evening on Sunday as we walked in the park. Little did I know that this was the point where my life would change completely. Under the setting sun, he told me that he would protect and love me.

Everything seemed in place at that time.

After such a long and exciting day, we got home, and all I wanted to do was shower and jump into bed. He kept insisting on taking a shower with me, but since I needed alone time, I refused. After all, I needed to process the roller coaster of emotions and events that had occurred in the previous days.

But his constant insistence finally made me put my guard down. I let him hop in the shower with me, and that was when I realized that during the whole trip, he never let me shower alone.

This thought comforted me.

The next morning was met with a surprise. He told me to wear something white that day, which made me suspicious.

Nevertheless, I did as I was told. We had breakfast together, and something about his attitude that day made me realize that he was going to marry me.

The day ahead of us had excitement and anticipation. He first took me to the mall to get matching outfits, and then we went to the beach. A romantic evening on the beach followed by anticipation of what the surprise was going to be. The waves glistened in the evening sun while the sky cast an orange and blue hue on the waters.

I was nervous.

He took me to the sandbar, where he dropped the question, "What would you say if I asked you to marry me?"

"I'd say yes," I already knew what was coming. But, the fear of holding onto hope made me ignore my excitement and focus on getting dessert.

The night was ending, and my nervousness was rising. And that was when he got down on one knee and proposed.

I was over the moon as I screamed a yes, and he put a finger on my hand, locking me for life.

Happiness is a minute word to describe what I was experiencing at the moment. It was utter bliss. And as I kissed him, I felt like I did the right thing. Time passed in Alabama as I broke the news to my family members and my kids. Everyone was happy for me and was ready to accept him as a family member with open arms. As for us, we were so comfortable with each other that my time there felt like it flew by.

Our endless conversations and compliments had to sadly come to an end in the second week of my stay in Alabama. He didn't want me to leave, but my responsibilities were calling for me. With all the appreciation that he had provided over time, I couldn't help but be smitten. He used to take me on dates every night and compliment me. He cared for me so much that I felt like I was living a dream. Things seemed to be turning my way, and I was enjoying myself.

Things went swiftly with him. Everything happened so suddenly that I started to wonder how I could fall for him so easily. It only took him giving me attention and calling me his wifey. I started trusting him and brought him back to Michigan to meet the kids. He had requested it himself, and I simply agreed. At that moment, I was blinded by all his affection towards me.

When we went back to my house, that's when things escalated. He started to talk about how he couldn't wait to marry me. So, we decided to tie the knot on September 8, 2022.

Our relationship, though with ups and downs, was fine for the most part. We were able to get over our differences, and our love increased over time. We were living together like one happy family, and life seemed to be coming around.

Right up until he started cheating on me, which is also when I finally realized how skilled at love bombing my second husband was.

In 2024, he started to have an affair with a coworker. He slowly started to remove himself from his homely responsibilities. He stopped paying the bills, and everything watered down on me. I had to start taking off the household chores and the finances. I had my suspicions about his whereabouts, but in February of 2024, I was deeply hurt when I found out about it. I was finally comfortable with my life, and God sent another test my way.

Everything was getting unbearable. My heart sank as I realized that my love for him didn't matter to him anymore. The affection, the appreciation, and the care disintegrated into the ground. I was hurt and disappointed. As soon as I got the news, I filed for divorce and got a personal protection order.

I didn't want to see his face anymore. It would remind me of all the good times we had had and how he was able to throw it all out just for a meaningless affair. It seemed like I was worthless in his eyes, like I didn't matter to him. And revisiting the past, the initial stages of our relationship just made everything seem like a lie. As if he never meant it and he had never loved me. I had found myself in the hands of betrayal. Trusting men seemed like a mistake.

I had found out about him cheating on me through reading his chats with a woman who was living with her parents. A woman with whom he had been having sex at work. He disrespected not just me but my love as well. The old wounds that had been stung by my first husband started to reappear in my heart. I had no choice but to swallow the bitter pill of acceptance and realized once again I'd been let down when it came to love.

Chapter 6: Joy Amidst Pain

Motherhood is an overwhelming position, to say the least. It is like a division of the self into several parts to deal with your issues and your children's needs. Difficult emotions are involved, and each strand of feeling that contributes to the experience makes life beautiful. It is a journey that doesn't simply involve unconditional love but hardships. Each moment is dedicated to meeting the needs of your children.

It is a hard position to be in, but it is given to a gifted few.

I am lucky enough to be one of those lucky people who got to experience motherhood. It all begins with the overwhelmingly beautiful and difficult experience of childbirth. It brings joy, pain, misunderstandings, and adjustments to accommodate a baby in your belly and your life. During childbirth, in those surreal moments when your baby is pushed out of your body, and you hear his cries for the first time, it dawns upon you that you are a mother now.

And that realization alone can lift up your emotions. But there is anxiety about the responsibilities ahead as well. Nevertheless, the experience is beautiful. For me, childbirth was like sunshine after rain. I had never felt so free and so happy in my life.

Even though my children mean the world to me, and they are one of the few sources of my happiness, my past trauma sometimes gets in the way of my raising.

I grew up in a turbulent household- A place where not only abuse took place but where I was forced to be in the position of an adult. I was a child, yet I had to suffer so much because of the limitations of my mother. She was not able to take care of me because of her issues.

So, when I look at my children, I see my childhood being projected onto them. I see a childhood that I want to add happiness to. My parents weren't able to provide me with happiness, so I made my younger self's dreams come true through them. They are my life and soul; I wouldn't change anything about them.

I try my best to give them a life I was never given. A life that I had every right over but wasn't provided due to my family's shortcomings.

There are a lot of emotions attached to motherhood. There is happiness when you see your children succeeding in life. There is anger when you notice that someone has hurt your children. When they are fearful, you shelter them. You become a counselor when they need suggestions, and when it comes down to love, there is an abundance of them.

There is a mixture of both exhaustion and exhilaration involved in this experience. There are sleepless nights and hard days when you forget to take care of yourself because your kids need you. The issues that lie in my past give me the strength to be the best version of myself for my kids. They deserve the world, and I must give it to them.

Every laugh and every cry of them puts me on high alert, for my maternal instincts are strong enough to pierce through any threat to my kids. They aren't the only ones who learn, but I also learn. Every day, they teach me something new about life and themselves.

My past traumas made me hyper-aware of my children. For instance, I remember my daughter's teacher calling me to let me know that she was having an asthma attack. Worried, sick, and panicking, I called the superintendent of the Detroit Public School and complained about the teacher not catering to my daughter's needs. I wasn't going to back down when she needed me the most. The teacher got fired because of how furious I was at the mistreatment, and she lost her pension as well.

When it comes to my kids, I don't let anyone get in the way of their safety and well-being.

My place always remains crowded. My kids, with their squeals and laughter, keep the house alive. I wouldn't be able to call it home without their presence.

We have fun, but we also set strict boundaries. I have made sure to discipline my kids. But in a way that it doesn't suffocate them. My past has made me more sympathetic toward them, although it would never hurt to be a little more understanding.

I have to be more attentive towards them because I am a single mother. The first divorce had left me in shambles, but this time around, I had faith by my side to help me out. I got through the divorce by praying. Going to church and believing in the light of God helped me from spiraling into addiction again. This time around, I had ambitions and goals to fulfill. So, diversion was the best solution for me.

I diverted my mind away from my divorce and my cheating ex-husband and onto productive thoughts. I started to think of the future of my kids and my own. I thanked God for the separation because I didn't want to be in a marriage in which I wasn't prioritized. It was clear that he didn't want me. His mind was elsewhere, so I decided to do the same. He didn't deserve any of my tears.

I felt like I had always been right about people. They aren't to be trusted. Expectations shatter all the time, but if trust breaks, the person is affected immensely.

I worked toward myself and my goals, pushing through the pain. I knew that there was no use in wasting my energy on a man who was never loyal in the first place. It was never about me; his shortcomings landed him in this mess. Partners who cheat are the worst kind of people to be around. So, it was best for me to end things there and then. I wasn't going to stick around to give him a second chance. I knew that if he was capable of cheating once, he was capable of doing it twice.

I had enough self-respect to leave him and move on with my life. He didn't deserve my love or appreciation. Husbands are supposed to take care of their wives and children. It is their duty to be grateful for the life they are gifted. Biblically, socially, and morally, it is the right of married women to question their husbands about their suspicious behavior. In Ephesians 5:33, it is mentioned that,

"However, each one of you also must love his wife as he loves himself, and the wife must respect her husband."

The mutual foundation of love and appreciation is what makes a relationship strong. My ex-husband, unfortunately, refused to understand the importance of holy matrimony. It is tragic, but I am glad I could get past him.

In getting over my divorce, I turned to trivial matters. I started to focus on my mental health, my children's well-being, and church. The aftermath of the divorce was ugly, but I transformed it into something positive. I had found myself at a crossroads, where I had the choice to be faithful to my religion and my kids or go back to my old turbulent ways.

To my ease, choose the right path. The path of light and Christ's intended for us to follow. God has created marriage to make people celebrate love for themselves and the love their Creator has for them. It is a union that is an emblem of mutual respect, sacrificial love, and commitment. My second husband defied the principles set for him and evaded his biblically prescribed duties as a man.

Another area where he lacked is communication. Communication is vital in marriage. You need to voice your opinions and concerns to your partner and let them know where you're coming from. Proverbs 15:1 reminds us that:

"A gentle answer turns away wrath, but a harsh word stirs up anger."

When communicating with your partner, it is necessary to use sympathy instead of aggression to conclude an argument healthily. I wasn't able to find any of that with my husband. All he did was be impatient and act suspiciously.

"Bear with each other and forgive one another if any of you has a grievance against someone. Forgive as the Lord forgave you." (Colossians 3:13)

Forgiveness is necessary for closure. In a healthy marriage, if conflicts arise, it is necessary to look past them and work your way towards a solution. It is a reminder to couples that there is a way to work things out.

A marriage will always have problems, but the couple needs to be grounded and devise a solution. If the fight doesn't de-escalate and you remain stubborn in your old ways, then you're not fit for this holy union.

Forgiveness allows healing on both ends; if you are too stubborn to understand this, separation becomes necessary. I think this is what happened between us. My husband was too rigid in his ways to look at me with sympathy. And even though I have forgiven him for my sake, I believe it is hard for people like him to change. I have also forgiven him because God has advised us to do so. This world is temporary; if we hold onto grudges, we'll be stuck in unhealthy ways forever.

In *Ephesians 4:32*, it is mentioned,

Be kind and compassionate to one another, forgiving each other, just as in Christ God forgave you."

Forgiveness supports and builds trust. In mine, though, there was none.

Marriage is a union that is supposed to be celebrated. The unity should embody the qualities that God intended for us to have. Sympathy, honesty, compassion, and love are some of the basics that should be a part of the marriage.

None of which I could find in mine.

I have no regrets, though. I believe I learned from this experience and became a better person. Despite the challenges and hurt I received, I learned and formed a deeper connection with my family and children. I also understood the importance of honesty in a relationship and hope to look out for it in the future.

The smiles and love for my children kept me alive and breathing in these learning moments. It provided me with hope. Their laughter could lift weary hearts and lighten even the most difficult days. When bringing up a big family solo as a parent, these illuminating moments were what kept me going.

Raising children on our own can be challenging, but the experience can be rewarding. Every day seems to be a balance between struggles and happiness. There were times of exhaustion and self-doubt. In such moments, I looked towards balancing my responsibilities. Yet, in the middle of this comes so much happiness and pride when you see your children grow, learn, and flourish. I saw them excel in their studies and sports each day, which filled my heart with pride.

It felt like I had taken a grip on my purpose in life.

The strength found in children's smiles is far from any simple, short-lived enjoyment; it's a strength able to win. They teach us patience and how to love without conditions truly.

In a large family, there is laughter, sadness, and hints of patience during hard times. In my hard times, my children were my source of solace. They kept me going.

Through it all, God was by my side and made my rewards abundant. Through the challenges was the light of smiles and meaningful conversations that made my hard work and maternal love worth it—the only condition for my love was seeing my kids happy.

This is what motherhood is all about.

From simple moments of chuckles during family dinners to the milestones one proudly celebrates, raising kids is one of the most difficult and rewarding tasks one could attempt. It instills values, imparts wisdom, and gives a sense of belonging.

Ultimately, whereas this path might be rough, the love and smiles of children light up the way ahead. They remind us that we are never really alone, even in solitude. In my moments of despair, I would turn to my children, and a smile would appear on my face. They are my everything. Their resilience reflected my own, and their laughter was sheltered.

Chapter 7: Seeking Solace

Faith kept me anchored, and the church proved to be a sanctuary throughout the process of trying to heal. Thankfully, even as I flailed through and suffered trauma, I was still able to be at peace and be strong in my belief in God. Whatever I suffered, the knowledge of the loving God and the wisdom in biblical scriptures helped me and guided me.

"He heals the brokenhearted and binds up their wounds."(Psalm 147:3)

I remember that verse; it used to speak volumes to me. So many times after my trauma, I felt that my heart could break into a million pieces. I clung to this promise: God was tending to my wounds, emotional or psychological, and somehow, it brought relief to feel that, somewhere, someone greater than me saw all this brokenness and was watching over it.

Church life became very instrumental in my healing. It provided a basis for interacting with people with similar values and experiences. The feeling of belonging was very comforting.

It made me realize that it is not all about attending services but about having people around you in times of need and also providing support.

"For where two or three are gathered together in my name, there am I in the midst of them." Matthew 18:20

Congregational worship made an integral part of my spiritual journey. I transitioned from feelings of loneliness to experiences of happiness through social settings.

It was very important for me to build a supportive community through the church and social activities. The healing from the trauma meant new ties and a sense of normalcy in the new place.

All activities conducted at the church, ranging from Bible study and prayer groups to volunteer work, have been instrumental enough in making me grow at both personal and social levels. These activities were much more than religious practices; they were opportunities to build important relationships.

Socializing and participating in activities outside the church helped me form a good support system. Being part of clubs, attending social functions, and involving myself in activities in the community made my circle large and widened my base of friends. This helped to reduce the feelings of loneliness and led one to a feeling of normalcy.

The pain given by my heartbreaks and turbulent childhood started to fade away. I had God by my side.

"A friend loves at all times, and a brother is born for a time of adversity." (Proverbs 17:17)

This is a verse that reminded me of the value of supportive friendships. Building those relationships, first in church and then in other social activities, gave me the firm power I now needed throughout my personal growth and healing.

Though much had been overcome through faith and the community's support, public appearances and social anxiety remained strong battlefields. The fact that these issues were prevalent was just a reminder of the trauma that I had gone through

"When I am afraid, I put my trust in you." (Psalm 56:3)

This verse most encouraged me in the fight against social anxiety. When I began learning to put my trust in God, my fear and anxiety were brought under control. It was through the normal cycle of prayer and asking for his help that I found the courage to push myself in social situations and gradually fight through the anxiety.

I was very proactive in my approach to handling my PTSD and night terrors. I knew I had to gain control over my mental health, so I opened up to a host of things. Self-care and praying helped me through this.

"Cast all your anxiety on him because he cares
for you."(1 Peter 5:7)

This verse proved to be very encouraging because it taught me how to cast all my anxieties upon the Lord. In my situation of dealing with PTSD, prayer and meditation became very instrumental and key in my healing. This helped me cast my anxieties on God, and I felt relieved and supported along the way.

Establishing a self-care routine was the most essential element. It called for working hard to have a constant routine that involved exercise, proper nutrition, enough sleep, and mindfulness techniques. This helped in creating that kind of stability and control over the symptoms of my PTSD.

Spiritual exercises supplemented these: reading scripture, listening to prayer, and attending church services. The consolation from these two components largely brought me peace, so to speak, and reassurance of the existence and the backup of a superior force in my life. They comprised a major portion of my thriving.

"The Lord will fight for you; you need only to be still." (Exodus 14:14)

That promise of God to protect and support gave me rest in the assurance that if He fought for me, it was all the support I needed. His strength was magnified through my weakness as I learned to rely on Him to make war in my place.

Faith and church life became central to my journey to healing, both in comfort and growth. Active participation in the church and building a community that could offer support meant rediscovering belonging and connection. Even though social anxiety and PTSD remained immense tasks, proactive steps and faith-based practices armed me with the tools to do so.

This healing journey was not one of straight lines, but with faith, community support, and deep caring for myself,

I was able to make it through the trauma maze and find a way out to a place of healing and personal growth. The guidance and comfort that scripture gave me, combined with having the loving church community as part of my support system, acted as a moral compass of hope and a source of strength in my healing process.

The church became a place of refuge for me. It was where I did not feel judgmental, and it was filled with the spirit of God every time I walked through the doors. Again, this was rather calm and serene—unlike anything I ever felt. I learned healing in the church and also sought new ways to approach my life or begin to study the Bible more profoundly.

The Bible turned into a soothing, protective guard and guide. I delved into its teachings to skillfully find my way through the difficulties that my life threw at me by its wisdom. What came with each scripture learned was a new view and a sense of assurance. With each reading and its understanding, I felt empowered to confront my struggles with faith. One of the verses that impacted me the most was,

"I can do all things through Christ who strengthens me." – (Philippians 4:13).

This divine promise became a foundation for my faith journey. It reminded me I was to fight battles in inhuman situations or surmount difficulties with Christ's strength.

A big part of my healing was building a community in my church. I surrounded myself with people who shared similar values and experiences. Everybody in that church was dealing with something, and I tried to get toward not holding it in, sharing, or connecting with those who could teach me different ways to cope with the trauma. I was around people who were supportive and knowledgeable about managing pain and healing.

I learned in that healing process that the same involved engaging others and not isolating myself, as I tended to do when I was self-conscious about what others said about me. Focusing helped me to socialize, and it was thus easy to chat while building new friends.

One of the key approaches to managing social anxiety was understanding how the thoughts affect the way I feel and act. I always realized that in my thinking, there would be characteristics linked to my anxiety paradigms of negative thinking and doubt. Understanding this enhanced how I attended to my anxiety issues. I confronted my negative thinking and replaced it with positive and realistic thinking.

Sleep has also become an important aspect of taking care of myself. I learned that proper rest must be managed to keep at bay my anxiety and mental state in general. Insufficient and disturbed sleep further exacerbated my anxiety, and the more open to the stressors and bad thoughts I had, the worse it got. When I started taking care of my sleeping habits and tried to have a regulated sleep schedule, I could feel an improvement in my mood and tolerate social situations better.

Another big lesson was practicing kindness to myself. While healing from trauma and managing anxiety, one aspect that played a great role was patience and self-compassion. I learned how to treat myself like a friend—kindly. This would include allowing myself grace for inevitable slips, recognizing growth, celebrating small wins, and reminding myself to live day by day. Being self-compassionate built up that muscle of resilience and kept me holding onto the positives during tough times.

My church support team has been very instrumental to me. They did offer a hand when I almost broke down, giving me advice and emotional support. They could well feel and understand my struggles, extending encouraging words, showing the way to support me, and showing the way out.

Therefore, being a part of a church community has made me realize that I am not at all the only one passing through the circumstances. It helped a lot, truthfully, to realize that others, too, were making their way through recovery and growth. Shared experiences and mutual support in the church made everyone feel united and in a place where they belonged. My faith strengthened because of the shared time that I gave others, which was a source of hope and comfort.

I eventually learned how to engage in real-time connections rather than just worrying about my fears while I was with others. By being involved with people and immersed in the church's activities, I found meaning and got a chance to establish relations. I would also learn from others who had gone through this and had become champions, pieces of information that inspired me and even gave me practical application of my challenges handling.

My faith and community journey made me realize that healing involves much more: spiritual growth and the practical steps taken toward managing mental health and developing supportive relationships. The combination of faith, self-awareness, and community support became imperative in my healing process.

As I shared and tried to practice these lessons with my church community, the significantly small but gradual development that had started coming my way really could not be unnoticed. My social anxiety levels began reducing quickly, and I found myself more confident when interacting with others. The sense of belonging and support received from the church was a source of great resoluteness and solace.

I am, of course, grateful that faith and community were there to help me get through my experience. Had it not for the underpinning of my faith and tangible and emotional support from the community church, then I wouldn't be in a position to consider the transformative nature of recovery as it happened. My faith offered me a base for recovery, while my church community gave me hands-on and emotional support to see me through the tough times of trauma, out of which I have come stronger and more resilient.

Today, I look back with pride at the journey I have gone through. At the first level, my healing and growth validated the power of faith and having a support network. These were my first sources of validation of faith to chart my life. All through it, I have learned that with faith and the right support, we can overcome even the most daunting challenges, finding a way to grow personally and remain fulfilled.

"Surely He has borne our griefs and carried our sorrows; yet we esteemed Him stricken, smitten by God, and afflicted. But He was wounded for our transgressions; He was bruised for our iniquities; the chastisement for our peace was upon Him, and by His stripes, we are healed." (Isaiah 53:4-5)

Chapter 8: Advocacy And Awareness

I came to a crossroads after my divorce. It gets harder to detach yourself from a person with whom you'd planned to share a life when you are so used to having this person around you at all times. This person who was supposed to be your anchor and your forever. Letting them go and detaching is challenging.

Life brings people into your life and takes some away. Despite the disappearance of some being a blessing, it still takes time to get used to the change. I had found myself feeling alone and left out when I signed the divorce papers. With freedom came a sense of change that had touched my life for a while. Being single again was thus a double-edged process. It has kept forcing me to step back and reflect upon my life, concentrating on what truly mattered in my life: my children, my well-being, and personal growth.

This journey was about learning to be myself again, finding happiness in the little things in life, and understanding what made me truly happy. The first one of those steps involved reconnecting with faith. Church was no longer merely a ritual but a haven for my soul.

The quiet time of reflection and prayer brought peace, reorganizing life in conjunction with spiritual values. I started to expose myself to the scripture to draw strength and guidance from the Bible.

Matthew 6:33 says, *"But seek first his kingdom and his righteousness, and all these things will be given to you as well."* This verse became a cornerstone of my journey. It reminded me to put my relationship with God first and seek His guidance about every little thing in my life. My problems were automatically taken care of when I focused on my faith.

The sense of comfort in the community was found within my church as spiritual growth continued. Understanding others with similar values helped me feel I belong and find support.

Conversation with fellow congregants was a social interaction and an opportunity for mutual encouragement and growth. We shared stories about our struggles and triumphs, and such sharing has aided me to feel less lonely in my journey.

I spent time contemplating my passions, interests, and dreams. It was that opportunity to explore what truly made me happy beyond the confinements of my previous roles and relationships.

"Trust in the Lord with all your heart and lean not on your understanding; in all your ways submit to him, and he will make your paths straight." (Proverbs 3:5-6)

This verse consoled me and taught me to always know God's plan for me even though I did not see the big picture. It was in that letting go of my expectations about my life and embracing an uncertain future that, for the first time, I felt like I knew where I was going. Being happy with myself became one of the most essential themes on this journey, and in that process, self-acceptance became important in cultivating a positive attitude.

I learned to cherish small victories, everyday things, and little moments of happiness. It started to be quality time with my children, enjoyable moments of a favorite pastime, or simply quiet evenings that I learned to appreciate all those little things that mean so much. Love and self-worth should be found within the Bible, too.

"We love because he first loved us." (John 4:19)

That somehow led me to think that I am worthy simply because God loves me, not because someone else said so. Understanding such a thing helped me find more depth in loving myself and fully accepting myself.

In the process of building a new self, relationships with people I loved became much closer to me. I nurtured the relations and found pleasure in spending time with family and friends. The supportive and loving people further reiterated how good it was that the circle of support was strong. Apart from personal growth, I began to dream and visualize a plan for the future.

What do I want to accomplish in life, and how will my actions contribute to turning these goals into reality? It could be higher education or career enhancement, building skills toward excellence, but all in all, an idealistic future vision would evoke a sense of fulfillment and values worth living for.

"May the God of hope fill you with all joy and peace as you trust in him, so that you may overflow with hope by the power of the Holy Spirit." (Romans 15:13)

With this verse, I embraced my life-building process with much hope, joy, and peace. It inspired me to remain optimistic and believe that God's guidance would bring me a bright future. This rediscovery of the self after change and self-discovery was multidimensional: I dealt with faith, reached out to my community, took social media positively, and concentrated on what made me happy. The lessons from the Bible guided and reassured one to trust in God's plan and find joy in the present moment. Therefore, through this process, I learned what self-love is, growth, and how relationships should be fostered. The happiness I finally found within myself, now focused on what truly mattered in life, made life far more meaningful and rewarding. These stepping from challenges to triumphs became stepping stones toward the future that I now authentically lead and embrace all the fullness of life's opportunities.

Other than challenges with my faith, I also found motherhood to be tough after the divorce. It was full of growth and extraordinary joy. And watching my children grow up has been one of the greatest thrills of my life. Each milestone they reach, each step closer to their ideal self, is a true testament to God's grace and guidance. This has taken a journey of perseverance and faith, and I have come to appreciate the blessing it is to witness their development and success. As I reflect on this journey, I can trace God's hand in every moment. From my early days in motherhood—when rearing my children all by myself was so tough—to the present, when I see them independent and working in their places, this has been a reminder of God's faithfulness and love.

My children growing and becoming independent gives me immense joy. Every accomplishment, no matter how small or large, makes my heart swell with pride and gratitude beyond words that *can be comprehended.*

"Children are a heritage from the Lord, offspring a reward from him." (Psalm 127:3)

I could not have found better words to describe my children. They are such a gift from God, whom I thank for giving me this golden chance to be his mom.

I have two grandkids with my oldest daughter, and one of my twins has also blessed me with a granddaughter. As for my 19-year-old son, he has a daughter as well. Having three granddaughters and a grandson, my life feels complete. It is full of love and appreciation for each other. On their birthday, we celebrate each other's special days together. We also take holiday trips and go out for park hangouts, the movies, and the beach.

It's been such a blessing to have been able to witness them growing into very strong, capable individuals. I often think of their ability to manage each situation and their strength as somewhat symbolic of the support and love through life's journey—similar to the depth of growth harnessed by us in times of turmoil. Being a single parent hasn't come without its struggles. It required strength, sacrifice, and faith. There were days when the feeling of uncertainty and questioning had become second nature, unsure if it was enough or the right choice for the kids.

However, in all that uncertainty and struggle, I found comfort in holding the belief that for every struggle God places before us, there is a purpose.

"And we know that in all things God works for the good of those who love him, who have been called according to his purpose." (Romans 8:28)

This verse has always been my beacon of hope in those tough and distressing times. It assures me that when things turn bleak, and one does not even know what is happening, God works behind the scenes for our good. I guess every difficult situation and every moment of self-doubt was part of a plan that would make one's growth and blessings possible.

I found this joy of life through my children and the joys that come with my children having children, my growing and growing. They are a crown of joy and pride indeed, but more to this, a symbol of the fruits of labored love to my very children into whom it was poured.

They remind me of the fulfillment of God's promise and the extension of his blessings towards our family. The experience of single parenthood has been a self-defining transformation. Being alone made me very sturdy, pushing the limits of resilience. I have learned to depend on God's strength and guidance in ways I never thought I could. Through trial and triumph, I have learned always to fathom God has a purpose for whatever happens in our lives. Even when I could not understand the reason behind things happening in a certain manner I had in mind, I hitherto kept faith that there was a divine plan. This is the verse in Jeremiah 29:11 that always keeps me going; it makes me full of hope and filled with heart every day:

"For I know the plans I have for you," declares the Lord, "plans to prosper you and not to harm you, plans to give you hope and a future."

This promise has been comforting and an encouragement. This allows me to think that, even in a situation where things are not very clear, God has hope-filled and promising plans for me and my family. I have learned to embrace this place and that there is joy in the now. Learn to trust God's plan in assurance of the fact that He does things for a reason; this enables me to be appreciative of my blessings and the path I'm on.

It has made me more appreciative of the little victories and more patient with the challenges. As is written in Philippians 4:13,

"I can do all this through him who gives me strength."

This verse has been a cornerstone of my faith and perseverance. It reminds me that all things are possible through God, and so are all the goals I set. This ranges from dealing with the challenges of single motherhood to being there to help my children overcome their problems and fulfilling myself personally. The way I think about it, it's God's strength through all this that enables me to keep going. I'm very optimistic and excited about the future because I know that God's leadership has taken and will continue to take me and my family into further growth and prosperity. The lessons and the blessings I had through my journey as a single mother made me strong and full of faith to face whatever may come next. My single-parent journey has been replete with great joy, growth, and increased faith.

It has been a blessing to see my children grow. I have learned about the blessings of God's grace and the importance of trusting His plan and finding joy today.

As for my extended family, we meet at reunions, funerals, and family gatherings. Though limited, each time I meet them, I am reminded of my physical resemblance with my mother. They tell me how much I look like her in my interactions with them. Since the thought of resembling a woman who had done me so wrong triggers me, I avoid excessively meeting them.

I will still trust in God's power and guidance daily, knowing He has a purpose in each step I walk. As I reflect on the past to contemplate the future, I am filled with hope and the assurance that all things are possible with God.

Living one day at a time has become one of the major rules in my life.

Every morning I wake up, I remind myself of living in the moment. This is more about commitment to little meaningful efforts than grand gestures, which need to be consistently upheld every night.

I knew that this was the very choice one makes, and after that, true growth comes, and well, I knew I was set to better myself by the day. The path toward getting into this frame of mind has been long and daunting.

It took me 30 years to realize that one important thing is to live in the present and not in the past. I used to dwell on the things that I had done wrongly and the opportunities I had missed and based my decisions on those. I have learned that everybody makes mistakes, yet my past need not dictate my future. I could be better only by focusing on what I can control today and thus working towards shaping a better future for myself. More specifically, one of the most salient lessons that I have learned is the power of surrounding oneself with people who uplift him or her.

I did meet many people who only tried to bring me down, but soon, I realized it had nothing to do with my worth but all about their insecurities and negativity. I've learned to distance myself from those people who make me feel bad or undermine my confidence. It is not about cutting people out of your life in an arbitrary way; it's a question of protecting your mental and emotional well-being. I would be able to trust how someone feels toward me if he shows it.

I have come to learn that people's words can be deceiving. If one person keeps disrespecting and treating me poorly, I would not let him keep on hurting me. Life is too short to spend time with people who don't value you or appreciate your existence.

This realization has helped me to build healthier relationships and surround myself with persons who contribute positively towards my life. It has been quite an eye-opener, realizing how life gives no second chances. I have started valuing the fact that time flies and how we must make the most of this by being productive daily.

My past experiences have taught me that life is unforeseeable, and one does not have a sure guarantee over it. This realization impels me to live to the fullest in the present and make decisions that are in tandem with my values and objectives.

Each day is a time for growth and improvement. It has been my practice to set small and achievable objectives for myself every day, which include personal development and relationships, among many others. By making such daily improvements, I can create momentum and even a sense of achievement that becomes self-encouraging.

These small steps add up over time to major strides in the right direction. I also remind myself to be compassionate toward myself. Some days, you slip up and don't do as well as you set yourself to, so I learned to let go of being hard on myself.

It has allowed me to recognize my efforts instead of moving on with more determination. It has allowed me to keep a positive perspective and stay focused on my journey of personal improvement. Besides the personal growth, being present and living for the now adds value to the relationships I have with people. By remaining mindful and being in the present with others, I enhance my relationships and allow myself to get deeply involved with others around me. I have enjoyed every moment spent with my loved ones and appreciate people in my life as a God-given gift.

The decision to live for today and improve me daily has done something miraculous to my perceptions of the world. I realized that the past is part of me, yet it is not supposed to dictate what happens to me in the future. Every day is another chance for a good change in life, and that is a great commitment to adhere to. Focusing on the present, I experience true fulfillment and happiness in the course of life as I try to make an effort to improve myself at all times.

The experiences of life have drawn my lines of living through the years. I have made principles out of living a day at a time, staying away from negativity, accepting people's actions, and savoring the present. The realization that life is so precious and each day counts as another opportunity to grow and do better. With these principles embraced in his own life, he strives to live a life of purpose, meaning, and fulfillment- a full life, enjoying every moment and working positively and tirelessly toward becoming an enhanced version of himself.

Chapter 9: Reflections and Moving Forward

As the pages of this personal memoir end, I want to look back at my life and all that I have been through. I remember only counting on my children and the Lord to push me out of dark times and carry me forward. They were a source of inspiration for me to become someone I see myself as today, proud of who I am.

I see my kids grow in their success daily, and pride fills my heart. God has made me the proud witness of the countless blessings around me. He made me the person I am today through my trials and tribulations.

The path to forgiving myself and others was perhaps the hardest part of my journey. It was like stepping into thorns and tearing through them to reach the light of faith, hope, and forgiveness. And I, never giving up on the process, finally reached the end of the road of thorns.

So long, I had been stuck with the wrongs that had been done to me in the past. I had built unhealthy coping mechanisms to deal with the everlasting pain of my existence. I was stuck in a constant cycle of hopeless degradations and didn't know how to avoid the pain.

That was until I found the light of faith.

Later, in quiet times, when I sat alone in my head, I finally began to understand that forgiveness is not an event but a process. There is no ultimate happiness I would fall into, and neither is positivity a permanent attachment. It's more of a process, to and fro, like the ocean's tides. There are days when the water is still, and I can see through, and there are days when it becomes agitated, and I struggle to keep my head above the waves. In learning to navigate these emotional currents, I have found that forgiveness has much less to do with an endpoint but much to do with a constant motion toward peace.

Forgiveness has so often required great strength, yet more often than not, it has come from the deepest places of vulnerability. Each person that I needed to forgive (whether they had wronged me or had wronged someone I cared about) became another challenge to confront my wounds. My heart began healing as I let go of the anger and resentment. I found solace in God's light and the Bible.

The process wasn't always smooth; there were those moments of regression when the past would trigger me. It would distort the image I would try to see, like a scratch on a plain glass surface. And so, I learned to live with it. I started to let go and started to pray more.

I remember how the divorces and heartbreaks had left me emptied of any emotions. I created walls around me to protect myself and forgot that outside, beyond what I saw, was God's love that I so desperately needed. I never realized how much I needed him until I started to pray for help.

This is all about accepting my imperfections and understanding that, as a human, mistakes are stitched to our souls. As long as we can pray for redemption, God will indeed listen to us.

My path of self-forgiveness was never about absolving myself of my guilt but about embracing my humanity and further growth.

It has been a very important part of the process of self-love and acceptance. It took me some time to rebuild my sense of self-worth after the trauma that was written in my fate. The trauma existed to make me the courageous person that I am today.

After the hardships, I often felt like I'd lost pieces of myself. Things that used to make me whole and vibrant felt so far away from me. The more I worked on loving myself, the more I realized those fragments of myself could be regained and nourished. I have learned to care for myself in the ways I had always wished others would: by speaking kindly, setting boundaries, and placing my and my children's needs first.

More important in self-acceptance is the realization that I am not my mistakes or traumas. My flaws don't shape me; they are a part of me that brings out my strength. My negatives make me realize how courageous and capable I truly am of wonder. I am defined by how I choose to respond and grow from negative experiences. It is through embracing my imperfections and understanding that, scars and all, I deserve love, which has become transformative for me.

Self-love and acceptance also meant letting go of the need for external validation. I spent a great deal of my life seeking others' approval, somehow believing it would fill the void inside. Yet, the real fulfillment came from inside. Validating myself and recognizing my worth began to build a stronger, more resilient sense of self. It has been a journey of discovering internal self-worth.

In learning to forgive and embracing self-love, I've found an inner peace of sorts. Not the type of peace dependent upon life going without hitches or problems, but acceptance of life's imperfections, knowing how I fit within these imperfections. Every day, I try a little more to forgive and reassure myself of my worth through the process. It is dance-graceful at times, clumsy, yet each time closer to harmony.

Both self-love and forgiveness require much patience, self-compassion, and exposure to new experiences that might seem daunting but can ultimately help you grow. In this process, I have learned that one does not need to erase the past to heal and find peace but to make room for growth and transformation. Each step forward, however small, is one toward greater insight into myself and a deeper connection with the world around me.

With healing comes the season of hope. Something that I have been looking forward to for so long. Hope is what ties humans to the thrill of life. As I pen down the last few pages of my autobiography, I see a bright future for myself.

Something that I want to strive for and find success in. Not just for myself but for my children, who have been with me through thick and thin.

My dreams, which consume most of my motivation for existence, are becoming a successful entrepreneur and writing books about my experiences. As for this one, it remains in a special place in my heart as it reminds me of where I started. The humble beginnings that I had to walk out of to climb the boulder of success and life.

I want to see myself successful in multiple areas, such as having that clothing line I want to launch. To achieve these ambitions, I want to be methodical and careful. From what I have learned over the years, taking life one step at a time is always the best way to go about it. Patience and achieving small bundles of success set you up for the ultimate success. I believe that if I set manageable milestones for myself and attend to one ambition at a time, I will eventually achieve all my dreams. My number one priority is finishing the book I'm working on. I am very much aware that this book may well prove to be one of the foundation accomplishments in my career, and I remind myself about my current state and where I want to be in a few years.

I now stand tall and independent, reflecting on a completely different version of myself two years ago. On my healing path, I have learned that it is important for me to be patient with myself as I build back my trust in myself. I know that some time is going to be needed before I fully regain my trust and self-esteem. Time can be the best healer, and with the help of prayers, one can find peace in the chaos of this life.

So far, I am convinced that reflecting upon my inner peace and self-improvement is just what I need to do at this stage. I also must continuously look out for myself because the Lord has created us with much love and care. It is only fair to treat this body like a vessel and filter through self-love.

Self-love has become part of my daily routine. Meditating regularly and praying more have brought about peace and a state of self-acceptance. I retreat to my prayer area every time I feel something negative is welling up inside me. It's there that I reflect on my journey from where I was to where I am now. I try to remember that *what does not kill me makes me stronger*, and I cling to that because I know I dare to fight.

For me, self-love is concentrating more on my happiness and self-fulfillment. It seems it has dawned upon me lately that nobody has to live with me but myself, so I need to make decisions that give me happiness and fulfillment. I have learned how people can have a lot to say about you when things do not go their way. Jealousy and envy surround you; therefore, there always is someone who wishes you ill. It made me keep personal matters to myself. Solitude has given me insight into self-awareness as well as reflection.

My support network is my close circle of friends and family, whom I treasure so much because, in many ways, they are all I have.

I make sure to take care of myself and be the person I always wanted to have around me to take care of me. This includes my hair, nails, toes, lashes, and eyebrows. I take myself out at least twice a month to dine at a nice restaurant, catch a movie, or visit a park. It's just a way of treating myself for the way I am. These individualistic experiences are for only me to enjoy. I must be there for the little girl or woman so afraid of life. Now that I have the means to treat her right, I do everything to see a smile in my reflection.

I've learned that I need to take care of what makes me happy because nobody else will. People can be problematic as they wear you down. No matter how dedicated you can be to people, the wrong crowd will always end up criticizing you. They can display jealousy and envy in so many different ways, and one must be aware of such situations and show grace while addressing such attacks. Keeping things private and only sharing with those who are supportive ensures peace.

In my journey of self-love, I discovered a significant thing about myself. I might be able to forgive people who have done me wrong, but I will certainly never forget the unjust treatment I received from them. My brother, who had abused me when I was young, or any of my husbands who have treated me wrong, might have a chance of being forgiven. However, forgetting the pain and the memories of struggle will never be erased from my memory.

For the sake of my heart and my self-respect, I keep my past in mind to move forward into the future. This ability has given me new importance in walking away from people, places, or situations that don't serve me in any more beneficial way for my life.

Every day allows me to be better than what I was the day before; that's what I mean by striving. So, my healing journey has genuinely made me stronger and wiser, which is something I am proud of. God was there with me throughout my journey, especially when I felt lost, hopeless, and lonely.

My experience reflects the drive to be the best one can be, just full of pride and accomplishment. Returning to where I was, I thought about how much I had developed and grown. Each challenge and experience molded me into who I am today, and I feel this gratitude for lessons learned. Self-improvement and personal growth still motivate me, and I look forward to the future.

"By His wounds, you have been healed." (1 Peter 2:24)